I0200791

Time Out

For

Happiness

Tom Molnar

Time Out for Happiness

Copyright © 2021 by Tom Molnar

All rights reserved. Except for brief passages quoted in newspaper, magazine, radio, television, or online reviews, no portion of this book may be reproduced, distributed, or transmitted in any form or by any means, electronic or mechanical, including photocopying, recording, or information storage or retrieval system, without the prior written permission of the publisher or author.

ISBN978-1-7343593-2-9

Apple Valley Press

To my wife, family and friends, without whose support a book like this could never have been conceived. To my wonderful editor, who does all she can to expunge any grammatical errors, and to those who read this book, that insights herein may serve to bring increased happiness into their lives.

Time Out for Happiness

"in all our troubles, my joy overflows" (Paul)

Not everyone grows up in a happy home with loving parents. I didn't. Today, most of us don't experience enough happiness in our daily lives. Anyone can feel downhearted. The key is knowing the ways to overcome our sadness.

Increasing happiness is much easier if we know how. Unfortunately, many of the ways commonly thought to bring happiness are wrong. This is proven by observation as well as by scientific studies.

This short book delivers insightful thinking on how to minimize sadness and increase joy. It features quick pick me ups as well as longer term strategies. Once we discard the ways that don't bring happiness and focus on those that do, like sharing with others, we will be well on our way to living a happier life. The truths found in this book are affirmed by those who have spent much of their working lives finding real answers to what brings happiness and joy.

Contents

Knowing the Difference Between Depression and Feeling Down

When reading a book like this it's important to know the difference between clinical depression and sad feelings. The former will need medical assistance. That is the preferred solution. Unfortunately, some of those who are depressed survive on alcohol and sometimes drugs. Despite all the advances in treatment services and therapies, it can be difficult to help such a person to realize that medical care and prescriptions are the best way going forward.

How does one know whether it is low spirits or depression? I can tell you, for unfortunately, depression is prevalent in my family. My aunt died in what was then called "an insane asylum." My mother could seldom see the bright side of things and became extremely depressed when my father died at a relatively young age. She became so severely depressed that her brother took her to California and enrolled her in various treatment programs to try to help her. All his efforts and all the treatments seemed to come to no avail.

On her return to Indiana, my sister found a place for her to live. My mother was able to care for herself in a minimal way if she lived near a grocery store that she could walk to. She didn't drive. You might wonder why neither of my sisters nor I took my mother in. If you have ever known someone who was extremely depressed, you might know the reason. Depression of that kind is contagious. One can feel it almost immediately when with such a person. Nothing you can say will lighten their mood. Instead, your own mood will darken.

My wife thought that when it was our turn to find Mom an apartment and be her guardian, that her cheeriness and banana bread would surely help. She was wrong. Just being around mom, bringing her to our home for dinners or taking her out to restaurants ended up being depressing. Despite our good intentions, my wife and I at times found ourselves arguing with each other when we were with her. Each time, after we had taken her back to her apartment and were on our own, we realized it was not so much us as it was her depression affecting us.

It was only later in my mother's life when my sister, who is a nurse, found a care facility for her that my mother's depression lightened. They were good to her at the nursing home, and besides, I'm sure they insisted that she take the antidepression medication. In those last years, my mother was better, and it is with great feeling that I remember her last days.

As you can see, my mother had real, severe clinical depression. There is a big difference between this long term state and major dejection that can affect anyone when everything goes wrong. I will make mention of such a major incident in my own life, only because it well illustrates the difference. You too, may also have had a devastating experience that, at least temporarily, took away all your joy. For me, it came this way.

After returning from US Army overseas duty, I finished college and then took two professional jobs, neither of which turned out well. So, I took a job driving a milk truck. Then, I met a girl. Our friendship deepened and in time we became engaged. I know she wanted me to have what she considered to be a "better job," and she had some connection with a major trucking company. As a result, I left the milkman job, even though the company offered me more money to stay. Things went well at first. I bought an engagement ring for her and together we bought a sofa that I kept at my apartment. Then, in November, suddenly things fell apart. I was laid off from the trucking company and almost immediately my fiancée broke off our engagement. She gave no reason.

I don't know why, but she wanted the engagement ring. So, she kept the ring and I kept the sofa. You can well imagine that I was depressed, suddenly finding myself with no job and no girl. My sister recommended that I see a psychological counselor. After one session with him, he told me that I was not clinically depressed, just very upset by difficult experiences.

Unfortunately, disappointments and even tragedies come into most of our lives. Usually, it will take some time for us to overcome major unfortunate events. Yet most of us will be able to do so. The insights presented in this book are likely to be helpful even after a tragedy.

Creating Our Own Reality

Leaving behind what makes us unhappy

Life is difficult enough without seeing and hearing about far away troubles. Yet newspapers, TV and the internet often focus on these things. The papers of large cities as well as local newspapers frequently headline murder, rape, and theft. Yes, we want to know of such things, especially if they are happening nearby. And it is also likely that the human mind tends to want to learn more of the details of why some people act so terribly. However, pursuing such interests can leave us with the feeling that the world is a bad place. This can definitely affect our happiness.

Each of us takes in the whole world, at least what we know about it, with two of our five senses. That is, our eyes and our ears. All of our vision and what we see of life comes through our pupils which are open only about 1/16th of an inch in bright daylight and about 1/3rd of an inch in relative darkness. In days long ago, in times that humans have lived since before antiquity, the eyes of human beings could only take in what was happening in and around one's village or town. However, since not long after the development of the printing press in 1440, flyers and newspapers have been able to announce goings on further away. This amounted to a revolution in the way we human beings could see the world.

Today, we are bombarded with news that comes to us from a huge variety of sources. Besides newspapers, we have radio, television, our cellphones and the internet bringing us news from all over our country and from all around the world. It's a lot for human beings to take in. In fact, there is no way that anyone can keep up with all that is going on in the world. We need to be selective of what we watch and what we hear. Unfortunately, if all we do is take in whatever is presented to us by media, we will tend to see a distressing image of our world. The reason? It is mostly crime, disaster and fatal accidents that is the subject of news. Yes, to an extent there is often some coverage of the good done by people and organizations, but usually such information gets only secondary coverage.

Fortunately, we can choose to what we will give our attention. While many TV shows and movies focus on violence and crime, other shows and movies show a lighter side of life. It's our choice, but it's important to know that what we choose does affect how we see the world. Many TV shows focus on local news and include, besides weather, some national and occasionally international news. Other programming gives in depth coverage of news of a political nature, usually with a slant toward one or another political party. Extensively watching these kinds of shows can be distressful, for these stations often go to great lengths to portray one side or the other in a favorable or unfavorable light.

There are some studies that indicate that people were happier in the "old days." Some of us may remember that in small towns everyone knew everybody. You knew who was cranky and who was good natured and you kept your eye out for someone suspected of being a thief. You could appreciate all the different personalities and from that maybe you came to be a pretty good judge of character. For most of us, those days are long gone. With air conditioning, we have no need to sit out on our porches, if we have one, on both nice and warm days. Many of us may seldom even see our neighbors, for we pull our vehicles into our garages and automatically close the door behind us. Perhaps fortunately, those who walk their dogs do get to see some of their neighbors and exchange simple greetings or talk more at length.

The point is that for many of us life has changed significantly from times when we knew the people in town or even in our own neighborhood. We still have our friends, people we've come to know through work, through school, through church or through any clubs or groups we have joined. Our friends are important to us and all evidence shows that friendships should be fostered both for physical and mental health. In fact, research shows that in general, those who live the longest have good social networks of people they care about including people who care about them. More to come later on what we can do to begin to create our own reality and thereby increase our happiness in life.

Screen Time

Ordinarily, those we work with and the family members we live with are those with whom we spend the most time. However, today, often more than time spent with people, time spent looking at screens has become more and more prevalent. Reportedly, teens, and young people as well as seniors, spend six and seven hours a day looking at the screens on TV, on computers, tablets and phones. These typically seated activities have been blamed for rising obesity rates. Currently, over two thirds of American adults are reportedly overweight and over a third are classified as obese. In addition, there is also a growing awareness among psychologists that the increase in overall screen time is cause for a significant increase in unhappiness.

It's easy to realize that sitting for long periods of time can lead to gaining weight. Those who have office jobs often spend almost the whole day seated. By and large, factory jobs have also been made physically easier. The heavier jobs are mostly handled by machinery. An easily noticed example is that in our area and perhaps in most towns, today an arm from the truck picks up the garbage and recyclables instead of human beings having to lift the contents of heavy containers into the truck.

But how is it that more screen time is thought to cause melancholy feelings? Almost all studies researching the matter show that it does. Especially so with those who spend a great many hours tuned in. But why? The answer, however, is not particularly clear. There is some speculation that time spent with screens is that much less time spent on real social interaction and face to face meeting with friends and associates. Also, with more time looking at screens, there is less activity in general, including such activities as walking, gardening, doing things around the house and participating in sports.

Screen time is almost always time that is spent sitting or even lying down. There is no doubt that the muscles of the body are designed for movement, and almost every study shows that exercise, even quite light exercise, is both physically and mentally good for us. It is likely hard to be unhappy or depressed when we are actively moving about and doing things. It is much easier to think unhappy thoughts when we are alone and doing nothing other than ruminating on all the things that bother us.

Perhaps the real danger of too much screen time is going with the flow. That is, allowing others to decide for us what they want us to watch. There is much in our culture that not only gives bad example to children and teens, but also can influence adults in negative ways. When one doesn't purposefully and deliberately choose on what to focus one's attention, others will choose for you what they think is important. The danger is that in time we may lose sight of what is meaningful and important to us. Often, those others who want to influence us are advertisers, trying to get us to buy their products. They may also be influencers who want us to think like they do. We can either make deliberate choices daily, or allow other people's agendas to influence how we think!

When one goes with the flow, passively taking in whatever appears on TV, on Facebook, on the internet, etc. we allow others to affect the parameters of our lives. Then, to some extent, we become a pawn of those who want us to act and think in certain ways. Fortunately, we have choices. We can easily switch channels or in other ways move to other sites of our own choosing. Or, we can turn off the power button and instead choose something we enjoy. Maybe music, maybe a project to start or continue, maybe play or watch a game or pick up a good book to read. We can leave behind the negativity and angst that is so often the content of national and local television and the internet. We have the power to choose, and it's an important power that relates to our happiness and how we see the world.

Our Calling

Our calling is maybe a loose term for what we do in life. Some of us try out different things before we hopefully end up with the type of job or calling that allows us to use our own individual talents. For teens and young adults, finding a calling can sometimes be difficult. Nobody wants to be stuck in a job they don't like. Further making things difficult for young people is the need to find a suitable spouse, particularly important as most of us choose to go through life in the married state. A good marriage can bring much happiness, a bad one, sorrow.

By the time we have reached twenty-five or thirty or so, we have hopefully settled into employment that pays the bills and gives us a certain amount of satisfaction. We are capable of doing the work our job entails and can do it well. We are recognized by our peers at being proficient or at least adequate at what we do. However, even when we are settled, there can be dissatisfaction with our employment. What we enjoyed doing early on in our job or career may no longer provide the same satisfaction as before. In our era of rapid technological advances, job duties often change. Even though our job title may remain unchanged, our job duties may be considerably altered. I personally found that to be the case when my company entered the computer age and personal contact with clients decreased while screen time using computers increased. Dissatisfied, I sought other employment, but in retrospect was glad I wasn't hired as my company later came out with a buyout program that enabled me to retire early with increased company benefits.

One way or another, it is important to find satisfaction in our working lives. Sometimes that may entail a change in our personal attitude, at other times a change of position or employment. As individuals, each of us has our own individual God-given talents and we tend to be happier when we can put them to good use.

Recognition (Fame) and Beauty

Happiness Killers

Besides money, it is probably unquestioned that for most people there seems to be a great need for recognition. From teens on, many of us feel a need to stand out from the crowd in one way or another. We see the competition to be the best in the Olympics and how motivating it is to strive competitively to be number one. Sometimes teens and those in their twenties achieve worldwide recognition by creating music that goes on to become internationally renowned. Unfortunately, achieving worldwide fame doesn't in itself bring happiness, as seen in the deaths through drug overdose or suicide of some of our most famous personalities. Such fame brings only temporary happiness, and then having to live in the limelight can make doing even ordinary things difficult due to being hounded by fans wherever one goes.

The need for recognition often shows itself in another more common way. That is in "conspicuous consumption." The dictionary defines this as "expenditure on or consumption of luxuries on a lavish scale in an attempt to enhance one's prestige." It seems that human beings, or at least a great many of us, easily acquire feelings of low self-esteem. We take to heart critical comments, whether they are made by our parents, friends, teachers or others. Buying expensive cars or pickups, expensive houses, getting all the toys— costly boats, swimming pools, winter homes, summer homes, and fashionable clothing, etc. may serve to increase our self esteem and show our friends and neighbors that we have arrived. However, research shows that these things do not bring happiness. Yes, it's true that for a short time a new major purchase may bring some excitement into our lives. However, studies show that major acquisitions do not in general bring long-term happiness. It has been tested and proven that even those who win a major lottery of a million dollars or more usually find themselves a year later no happier than they were before. Once our basic need for money is met, a substantial increase does not ordinarily bring more happiness.

The same can be said of beauty and physical attractiveness. We may tend to look at others and measure our own attractiveness in relation to others. Even in high school, we may look to see the beauty or handsomeness of others and sometimes compare ourselves negatively to them. Teenage years in particular can be difficult for many. Young adults may not have really found themselves, not settled into a calling or what they will do with their lives, and yet like all human beings, they feel the need to be loved and recognized. Personally, I always believed I was one of the "uncoolest" guys around. I know uncoolest is not really a word, but you know what I mean. I had rather low self esteem. Even when my future wife told me I was handsome, I thought it was only her love for me talking. However, now, when I look back at old pictures, I see that I wasn't bad looking at all, maybe even handsome back then.

Of course, the desire for personal beauty or handsomeness continues long after high school, and, in fact, for much of the rest of our lives. For women, the desire for expensive clothing, hairdos and jewelry can be very important. Men like to be fit, and some go to great lengths to achieve through weight lifting the powerful image of masculinity that some women find attractive. Others of us are happy to keep a modicum of fitness in different ways, while great numbers of Americans become portly by middle age.

In truth, beauty is another of the qualities that in itself does not bring happiness even though an entire industry has grown to remove wrinkles and lift skin to make us appear younger than we are. Beauty has to do with outside appearances, while happiness comes from inside. However, probably every one of us can appreciate someone we know saying, "Wow! Don't you look great today."

Materialism

"We live in a material world, and I'm a material girl."

It's true, as Madonna expressed in her popular song. We've always lived in a material world. And in order to get along in the world we need material things. This is especially true in cold climates where we couldn't live without warm houses or move about with any comfort without warm automobiles. Yet some people complain that we have become "too materialistic."

It's a fact that in the United States we are continually bombarded with advertising. Newspapers, magazines, and the internet are filled with ads, often taking up more space than news and articles. On television, ads of all kinds play as scheduled, as well as during game timeouts, injuries, and reviews of plays. I have read that the actual playing time for a full NFL football game amounts to only about ten minutes, if you take out all the huddles, time outs, replays and commercial breaks. My brother-in-law, a big sports fan, keeps his remote in hand and mutes all the commercials. I'm starting to do that too. Even our email accounts bring us commercials of what advertisers want us to buy. Those who write the ads are smart. They are able to design ads that appeal to our natural human desires. Sometimes they tell us in so many words that, "we're worth it," breaking down our resistance to making major purchases. A full-page ad that has been running in our local newspaper encourages the purchase of a quite expensive auto with the heading, "Don't drive ordinary."

Materialism can have many aspects. People need money to be able to live in modern society without too much worry. Those who barely scrape by, who are concerned about how to pay bills, may not be as happy in their life situation as those who have money in the bank and adequate finances to pay all expenses. So, in truth, happiness may depend at least in part on money. Those who have more than enough income and resources should theoretically be happier. However, such is not always the case. In fact, the doubling of income or even winning the lottery has been found not to increase happiness over the long term. Yes, winning is initially exciting, but not after some time has passed.

Studies indicate, that once a person or family has adequate income to take care of expenses, how extra money is spent is significant for happiness. What doesn't seem to help is working long hours and then spending more waking hours calculating how to make additional income far above what is needed for day to day living expenses. A parent who is always at work runs the risk of shortchanging family members with his or her presence and love. Unfortunately, it frequently happens that many successful people find that their marriages fall apart. Is it because they spend too much time on business and not enough time with family?

Success can be inebriating when others are telling us in so many ways how great we are. Whether we are recognized for our business acumen, our political power, or for our celebrity status, there is, I'm sure, a great temptation to cater to the whims of those who acknowledge our greatness rather than to be present in a meaningful way to spouse and family. However, fame is often fleeting and one can't hug a crowd. In the long term, the faithful and deep love of spouse and family is far more satisfying and brings much more happiness.

Spending Money on Happiness

Those who have an adequate to higher than average income can choose to use their extra income to increase happiness. Studies show that it is not <u>things</u> that bring happiness. Yes, a new car or house or something else can bring short term happiness, but after a while the excitement is over and the norm is to return to our previous state of relative happiness or unhappiness.

The question one might ask is, can money bring us happiness? The answer seems to be yes. However, not in the way that one might think, that is not in buying objects like fancy clothes, expensive jewelry, cars or homes. Studies show that an overall increase in happiness is found by spending on things that will help others. Donating to charities and to people in need is shown to elevate the spirits of both the giver and receiver. A person generous to others brings happiness to himself/herself.

Other studies show that experiences rather than things bring us happiness. Taking a trip to explore the greatness of America or foreign lands makes for happy memories that tend to stay with us long after the trip is over. Getting a boat for fishing or just for fun, or a bicycle or motorcycle brings us into outdoor experiences where we can leave the cares of the world behind. Even more mundane things like attending concerts, theater, major or minor sporting events and exhibitions (if of interest to us) are experiences that tend to raise our level of happiness. Studies show that doing things, rather than having things increases enjoyment. There are lots of great things to do in the world, and probably near where we live. Nature, for one thing, is beautiful in most if not all seasons of the year. We might do well to go out and enjoy it.

Some Major Causes of Unhappiness

Reasons for our unhappiness can begin early, in childhood. If we wish, we can assign some blame to our parents. Though most parents mean well when raising us, only very enlightened parents refrain from some common practices. It may not seem unusual for parents to say, "What's wrong with you," when children are slow to act or don't understand. Said enough times, it can be easy for children to assume that "something" is wrong with them. This alone can give rise to children having a low self-image that may continue long into adulthood, contributing significantly to unhappiness.

Of course, as children, we have no idea of what that "something" might be. However, we may easily perceive ourselves to be slow or not very bright. Besides parents, teachers may also say things to us that we may remember all our lives. My wife remembers well how a teacher said to her something to the effect that "your son is certainly not like your daughter," whom she had taught two years before. Yes, our son was not nearly as eager to shine and to please the teacher. He had his own way. He was in general a good student, especially in the subjects that interested him. Now, he is a college professor, Dr. Molnar. Rightly or wrongly, teachers often judge us, as do many others.

We also know that our experience with other children when we are growing up can cause us to retain negative images of ourselves. Kids can be mean, even cruel. Often, they can see our weaknesses and point them out. And, of course, they can be bullies. I felt the need to fight more than once in grade school, but afterwards, the bullies left me alone. Still, I knew that I was different in some way. Not a pleasant thought when one is trying to fit in.

The reality is that we are all different. Maybe it is only later in life that we learn to appreciate our differences. One thing from childhood that stayed with me the rest of my life was when a ten year old cub scout whom I thought was a friend called me "hatchet face." It's true, my head is widest at the top and narrows down to my chin. How could anyone be nice looking or attractive with a face like that? That appellation, "hatchet face" stayed with me for most of my life. It is only more recently when I've looked that I notice many people have the same type of head. Some, rather nice looking. But the damage was already done to my psyche.

The point is, we carry things from our childhood that can affect our self image and happiness for the rest of our lives. Even as adults, we are sensitive to what others say about us. A popular singer was concerned about her freckles. As she says in a song, "I used to care so much about what others think about, almost didn't have a thought of my own." Later, in the song she sings, "Cause a face without freckles is like a sky without the stars, why waste a second not loving who you are?" That's how we need to be. Admittedly, it's harder when we are young not to listen to those who in one way or another put us down. Yet we need to realize that each of us is different and just as there are a profusion of different kinds of beautiful flowers, so it is with human beings. We express our individual attractiveness in a multitude of different ways.

Moving Toward Happiness

Now that we've looked at some things that can have a negative effect on our happiness, let's take a look at some of those that can have a positive effect. To begin, I should note that there is research indicating that each of us is born with a "set point" of happiness. This comes from our genes, inherited through our mother and father. *("Thomas J Bouchard Jr.: Psychology: University of Minnesota" psych.umn.edu. Retrieved October 23, 2015,* and, *Lyubomirsky, and, Sheldon, & Schkade, 2005)* This finding certainly doesn't mean we are doomed to be either unhappy or happy in life. What it does mean is that based on genetics we begin our search for happiness at a different place. In truth, for those genetically blessed, happiness may come easier than for others. We see this in families. We all likely know households where argumentative discourse seems the norm in family interaction, and other families where a harsh word is seldom spoken. In both we often see long term lasting marriages. Likewise, we know people for whom the cup is half full and those for whom the cup is half empty. Those are like setpoints, and knowing our friends, we may have a pretty good idea of how they will react to news. Some will initially see the up side and others will see the down side.

Nevertheless, regardless of which group we belong to, or a blend of the two, there are definite ways that have been found to increase happiness. Two have already been mentioned, although briefly. They are exercise, and having a close circle of friends and/or relatives. It has long been known that regular exercise, and the US Department of Health and Human Services recommends 150 minutes a week, contributes to longevity. Studies show that exercise also contributes to happiness. Here's what Athletico Physical Therapy says of it, "When we exercise, the body releases chemicals that boost your sense of well-being and suppress hormones that cause stress and anxiety. Among the chemicals released are endorphins, serotonin and dopamine neurotransmitters which are related to pain and depression emotions." It is clear from this, and is shown in many other studies that chemicals that cause good feelings are released when we exercise. Even a short stroll can improve one's mood. In addition, the University of Vermont has found that just 20 minutes of any kind of exercise can boost one's mood for up to the next 12 hours.

Not everyone likes to exercise, though we may know that it is good for us. For some, exercise can cause pain. I don't think anyone should exercise to the extent that it causes more than fleeting pain. For myself, I'm a big fan of exercising regularly, and sometimes notice a little pain in my ankle or knee, etc. that goes away as I continue walking outdoors or on the treadmill. Of course, those who take up vigorous exercise and are not used to it will likely have some muscle soreness the next day. Normally, with regular exercise those feelings go away or are very much minimized.

So, that being said, exercise is definitely one good way to increase our general level of satisfaction and happiness. Probably just the fact that we have done something on our own known to be good for us is in itself cause for us to feel an increased sense of personal satisfaction. Exercise may not be the easiest thing to do, but having done it, we know we have accomplished something. As doctors and athletic trainers recommend, and I second, if you're just starting out, start out relatively slowly and increase as you become more used to it. Studies show that even minimal exertion is psychologically beneficial and more is better. Once started, don't give up on it.

As mentioned, a second general way leading to happiness is to have a circle of friends and family in whose company we feel comfortable. However, not all such small communities are equal. There is discord in many families and extended families, and whether one has a small or large circle of friends, some are found to be better than others. One of our best babysitters came from a family situation that was far from ideal. I came to realize that the girl's mother was a heavy drinker. Then I saw that when the woman was with some of her friends, she was critical of many things, including her husband whom I knew to be a good man. Such small groups, ones that focus on all the wrong things in the world and are even critical of family members, are not likely to raise one's level of happiness.

So, what does one do if one is a member of a distressed family? At our house, with four children and then my wife's father, who also came to live with us, we found the perfect sign for our refrigerator. "Our family puts the fun in dysfunctional." But all kidding aside, many families are hurting with breakup and bad feelings. We can try to ameliorate the situation by kindness and a show of goodwill, but long standing negative feelings in certain family members can become ingrained and are usually difficult to change.

Let me tell you about a friend of mine who currently has practically no family. She married a man for whom it was his second and her first marriage. Their marriage lasted for decades until he died. A year or so later, the only child of their marriage also died. This woman has a brother who lives a thousand miles away, but no other family nearby. You might think that after two deaths she would be depressed. Of course, she was greatly saddened by both. Her brother came to town for the funeral of her son, and he suggested to her that she move down south to be with him where she would at least be near part of her family. However, at the funeral and the gathering after, her brother changed his mind, saying to her something to the effect, "I can see that you have so many dear friends here; now I understand why you wouldn't want to move."

How did she do it? A retired teacher, she had retained friends from her school, and quite active in her church, she has many friends from there as well. Besides, she volunteers some of her time with an organization that assists needy women and provides food monthly to those in need. To me, she is an example of a woman who despite tragedy keeps busy and has many joys in her life. I am glad to be one of her many friends.

We all need friends, and we thrive on good family relationships. Some of us are naturally more outgoing than others, making good friendships easier to obtain. Others of us, not so outgoing, can join any of a great number of clubs and groups according to our interests. Very often, in such groups, we share not only interests, but we also make friends. If we have time, it's often good to check out various groups, and stick with one or two that we find to be the most enjoyable.

Another very satisfying endeavor for many, if not most of us, is to have a hobby or pastime. It is simply amazing to me the great variety of interests that we human beings have. These are things we enjoy doing, and often become very competent at, that tend to bring us satisfaction and happiness. Many women enjoy sewing or crocheting, making clothing, household items, afghans, sweaters, hats, etc. and giving them away. Friends and family are generally quite appreciative of such gifts, and those who have learned such skills can take satisfaction knowing they are able to accomplish something both utilitarian and also beautiful.

A relative of ours makes beautiful woodwork, even a full sized grandfather clock, and another makes bowls and all kinds of household things also out of wood. A friend waxes eloquent on how he is sometimes moved by singing in a church choir and a relative enjoys singing with a group with no church connection. Another, a self taught guitarist, actually makes guitars, and another makes beautiful stained glass pieces and gifts them to friends. The stained glass, we hang on a window, and another we put on our Christmas tree in season. Creating things with our hands, including baking cookies, candy or delicious bread that we can serve to our family and sometimes give to friends is satisfying in so many ways.

Personally, I like to write, and starting with friends and family, I find it tremendously encouraging when people are pleased with my writing. If you have such an interest, there are usually writing groups nearby which are helpful early on to hone one's skill.

For a long time, I was also interested in astronomy, and, of course, there are groups for that as well. Sitting out under the stars with like minded people and looking at the wonders of our universe through telescopes is satisfying, to say the least.

The point is, we can achieve happiness in learning a skill, especially if we can share it with others or even gift some of our creations to those who appreciate them. And it doesn't matter too much what kind of skill it is. Learning to paint or draw, learning to play an instrument, learning a craft or skill, even learning a new language, are only a few of the things that can bring us personal satisfaction and happiness. Human beings are by nature creative, and when we tap into some of our creative powers, we naturally feel a sense of accomplishment.

Removing the Negatives

Low Self-Esteem, High Self-Esteem, Humility and Pride

The way we see ourselves definitely relates to happiness. Although Christians are admonished to be humble, such humility may not be the kind of humility that comes to mind. Jesus certainly wasn't a picture of humility when he made a whip of cords and threw out the money changers in the temple.

Humility does relate directly to its opposite, pride, but not directly to self-esteem. Low self-esteem is not good. In fact, low self-esteem is not related to happiness but rather to unhappiness. I know this can be a bit confusing if you haven't thought about it in this way. Because these distinctions are important for happiness, let's take a look at them one by one.

Pride and apparent high self-esteem: We all know people who have too much self pride in themselves. They tend to do more of the talking, often cut others off, think they have all the answers, and often like to impress with their clothes, cars and other material things. Very often, they put people down, and also may tend to make fun of others. In their presence, you might have the uncomfortable feeling that when you're not around, they may make fun of you or something about you as well. Are they happy? No, not really. The fact that they criticize and belittle others shows that in reality they lack self-esteem. They try to build up their own esteem by putting down others so they can see themselves as better than others. This is not a happy way to live. In biblical times, the Pharisees were prime examples of people of this kind.

Pride and low self-esteem: This is the condition of more people than we may realize. In, fact, both you and I may currently or in the past have personally experienced this condition. Unlike those who are obviously proud, we don't like to stand out, and many of us feel uncomfortable to be on a stage or to have to address an audience. And yet, in many ways we are proud. We are quietly proud of our own successes and accomplishments. And, at the same time, we may be envious at the good fortune or affluence of others. We may wish that we were the one to receive the reward, commendation, or promotion. We may feel that another doesn't deserve what they have received, and instead we should have it. We may also feel that our worth and abilities go unrecognized. And here's the reality. Much of what we are thinking may be accurate.   It   often happens that those who are the most popular or well connected are the ones who are recognized. This, despite that others may be more capable or knowledgeable. I think those of us without high esteem may have noted that this happens. That we are passed over in these and in many other ways may well be a cause of unhappiness. Yet, unhappiness need not be the outcome, as will soon become apparent.

Humility with low self-esteem: This condition might well be thought to be the best. Isn't humility what the church and the Bible recommend? And doesn't low esteem go right along with humility? No, it doesn't, and this is why not. There are different degrees of low esteem. A person with truly low esteem has no confidence and always tends to put his or her self down. Such a person compares themselves to others and feels their lack in the comparison. Quiet, afraid to contribute much to a conversation, they have a very low opinion of their talents and abilities. Even if someone compliments them in one way or another or remarks on their good qualities or how they have done something well, the person with low self-esteem tends not to believe the compliments.

Unfortunately, though such a person may be called humble, it is not a desirable type of humility. Their low self-esteem prevents them from expressing their views when with others, especially when they find themselves in disagreement. People with low self-esteem are timid people, afraid to try new things, and unable to realistically acknowledge their own God given talents and abilities. Such people find little happiness in life and tend easily toward depression.

Humble with high self-esteem, the ideal: Humility along with high self esteem brings contentment and happiness. And, it is certainly not against the precepts of Christianity. In fact, to paraphrase Christ, he gave as the two most important commandments to "love God," and to "love your neighbor as yourself." In contrast to low self esteem, we are to <u>love</u> ourselves well so that we can appreciate and love our neighbor well. This doesn't mean pride, not at all. What it does mean is that we are to recognize the goodness in ourselves which will help us to see the goodness in others. And, it also means that we can be just as forgiving of ourselves when we make mistakes as we can of others. It means taking notice of our own talents and skills, we all have them, so that we can better appreciate the talents and skills of others.

Unlike the proud person, who is often envious of the successes of others, the humble person whose self esteem is based on reality is able to rejoice in the successes of another. Also, unlike the proud person, one who is humble with esteem has no need to prove their self worth by ostentatious display of wealth or erudition. Such a person is comfortable in their own skin, so to speak, and by almost completely forgetting self, can easily rejoice in another's happiness, or just as easily commiserate with one who is experiencing adversity.

This kind of freedom from negative thinking is likely what we all want and yet we may have some misgivings about it. We may even know a person who seems almost always perpetually happy and privately wonder if he or she is "on something." Of course, in that regard, we need to recognize that we are not all of the "social butterfly" type who is outwardly expressive of happiness. I know a person like that and can appreciate how effective she is in dealing with clients who need assistance. However, that is not me, and likely not you either. We typically express happiness in ways that are not so effusive.

How does one attain this freedom that comes from a state of humility along with high self esteem? It comes by recognizing all the good that is in us, minus our faults, and giving thanks. We need to recognize that as human beings we are created so far above all the other creatures of the world that nothing else can compare to us. No other creature can think, plan, create, and do what we can. No earthly creature could even dream of making an automobile, a telephone or a computer. We need to give thanks for the power of our minds and our creativity. Let's rejoice in all that we are able to do, and not belittle ourselves and act as if we can do nothing.

Here's the important thing, so that we don't become proud. It is important to recognize that our skills and abilities are gifts. They are God given gifts that make us different from one another and in that way allow us to share with each other. Yes, it's true, one may have studied long and hard to become proficient in a profession, but the ability to be able to do so is a gift, a gift for which one should be grateful. One may have a beautiful voice, another may be talented in playing a musical instrument, and another at handling all the myriad details of a project, etc.

We all have various talents, whether it be in business, in the trades, or in interpersonal relationships, to name a few. Knowing that our abilities and skills are God given, they are nothing to boast about, but rather to be used for our own benefit and to be helpful for others. We don't call a lawyer if our roof is leaking, or schedule a dental appointment if our car engine light comes on. No, we should be thankful that there are skilled people in many, many different areas, and recognize that in one way or another we also have skills that others don't have that can be beneficial to others.

Four Scenarios

As mentioned, the way we see the world has much to do with our happiness. If we are living alone, or in a difficult marriage or have troublesome children, our happiness can be much affected. In a general way, let's take these kinds of life situations one at a time.

Teen and Up Years

Despite the ebullience and energy of youth, growing up physically and emotionally is not generally easy. As teens and young adults, we tend to get so enthused, and also often so depressed. Especially when younger, we live in an in between world. Even our own parents will sometimes treat us like children and at other times tell us to "grow up!"

We may begin to realize that the world offers us many possibilities, but if we don't yet know what we want to do, it can become quite perplexing to sort out what to choose for a profession or calling. This too, is made more difficult in modern times. In days past, the most usual and common thing for a son to do was to follow in his father's footsteps. A farmer's son became a farmer, a carpenter's son, a carpenter, and a blacksmith's son usually continued the family profession. There was no confusion about what one was going to do in life, and having assisted your father since you were a child, you knew exactly what to expect.

For girls and women, the transition to adult life and duties was in those days in many ways even easier. Until the last hundred years or so, the vast majority of women stayed at home where there was always plenty to do with tending to children, cooking family meals, doing laundry and sewing in the complete absence of modern appliances that have revolutionized the kitchen and laundry. It was hard work. However, modern life has not necessarily made things easier for women. Most are expected to earn money with some kind of job or career, while at the same time caring for children as well as taking care of domestic chores. Cooking, cleaning and laundry often falls to the woman of the house although today more men are lending a hand. For a woman to have to do everything is certainly not an easy undertaking. Making things more difficult for both young men and women is the need to choose a job or career quite often without having the opportunity to experience what such employment is really like.

In addition to settling on an occupation or career, the other major need is to find satisfaction in life. The celibacy still required for the Catholic callings of priest, brother and sister is not sought after by most, the majority of whom seek to find their happiness in marriage. Today, probably more than any other time in history, we are so individualistic that finding a suitable partner can be difficult. However, there is joy in finding that certain person with whom one can hopefully spend the rest of one's life.

The Middle Years of Life

These tend to be busy years. Especially so, if raising children. Parents find that their children as they grow older tend to be increasingly self motivated and in ways that may be different from the way in which they were brought up. They are getting other ideas from their friends and from society and they want to try things out. It's important that we try to keep them out of danger and from experimenting with things that we know are likely to hurt them. Yet, as they grow older, it is very much the truth that they have minds of their own. As much as we might like to, we cannot control everything in their lives. We do the best we can by our children.

At our employment, as well, we may find increasing responsibilities. Husband and wife may find themselves going in different directions in their work lives. It may at times be a challenge to find meaningful time for just the two of you, but it is essential to do so. When children have left the home, and work obligations come to an end, ordinarily it is the husband and wife who remain. It is important to be on good terms with the one who will hopefully remain with you until the end.

Retired, Living Alone

When one lives alone without having to go to a job and meeting other people, one's happiness is very much dependent on oneself. A spouse may have died, leaving one single, or other circumstances like divorce may have led to one living alone. Others never married. There is little doubt that being the only person in the house can lead to loneliness. However, for such a person, especially one in reasonably good health, much is dependent on how the situation is handled. We need to reach out to friends and relatives to share time and conversation and sometimes go to events or to the theater. Seniors can also volunteer in a great many different capacities. In most towns, organizations exist that can help to channel one's energies to be of assistance in a great number of various ways. Being able to help others inspires good feelings. I am reminded of my older aunt, who even into her early nineties, helped friends by driving them to their medical appointments.

As mentioned, world and local news is often filled with angst and violence. A person living alone who spends a good part of his or her day watching many of the news channels is likely to see the world as a mean and difficult place. Seeing so much violence on TV may even make a person afraid to step out in the evening hours. The solution is to turn away from all the violence and tune in to other shows or to listen to music. Unless one really does live in a violent neighborhood, most towns and cities of America don't turn violent at night.

A Most Difficult Scenario

There is another situation that some of us might find ourselves in. That is, of being a caregiver. Such a situation can be relatively easy or very difficult. If the person we are caring for needs only temporary assistance while they are on the mend, we may be happy to provide it. If our loved one is on a course that will only lead to eventual death, that can be much more difficult. Depending on our own age and physical condition, we may or may not be able to provide all the necessary care. I know one family that splits up the care of an invalid mother among the children, each taking a couple of days to provide assistance.

Even more difficult is caring for a person suffering from dementia or Alzheimer's. It frequently happens that one or the other sees her or his spouse sinking into the later stages of the disease. At some point, they may no longer even recognize their own spouse. This is tragic for the one who is left behind.

The loss of a spouse in this manner can be one of the most depressing things anyone may ever go through. It becomes imperative to reach out for help from family, friends and professionals. Ultimately, if possible, arranging for the care of a loved one at a nursing home may be the best solution. There, he or she can still be visited while their condition is monitored by caregivers and professional staff. Life will go on, despite our grief and loss, and allowing ourselves to fall into depression is not helpful to anyone. Christians can take comfort in the knowledge that with God there is ultimately a far better place for us and our loved ones where all our afflictions disappear and our joy will be complete.

Quick, and not so Quick Pickups

No one wants to feel down, at least not for long. Below are some ways to leave bad feelings behind. However, one caveat. Sometimes, there are definite reasons for not feeling right. If we have hurt someone, have cheated or defrauded anyone, or said mean, untruthful or libelous things, remorse kicks in. Even those who have no religion and no belief still have a conscience. And, if we have wronged someone, usually our conscience will let us know. The thing is, our conscience is not all that specific. It won't automatically list our wrongdoings. Often, we will need to think things through to come to why our conscience is bothering us and why we feel sad about it. Once we can resolve the issue(s) with our conscience, we can begin to try to make amends. Then, we will feel better.

Otherwise, here are some good ways to overcome unhappiness.

1) **Gratitude**. As much as we may tend to think of ourselves as self made, the opposite is true. Each of us has so much to be grateful for. It begins with our parents. As good or not good as they may have been, we could not have survived without them. If like most, our parents loved us, we have so much more to be grateful for. Take time to visit them and talk with them if they haven't passed.

Next, we should be grateful for all the good things in life. Like sunshine breaking through a cloudy day, the aroma and taste of coffee or tea, the warmth of our home in winter or its coolness in the heat of summer with air conditioning, and that we have good food to eat. And, let's not forget to be grateful for friends and loved ones. We need to say "thank you" at times for all those who make our life easier and who bring contentment into our lives. It's easily done, in person, by texting, email, or even by sending a note by mail. Gratitude is usually much appreciated by those on the receiving end, and is known to also increase the happiness of the one extending it.

2) **Kindness**. Practicing kindness is probably the easiest thing we can do and the most fun. Not only that, the very act of doing it bucks up our self esteem because it shows that we have power—to do things for others. Kindness is easy, letting a car into our lane, or letting a shopper with only a few items go before us in line is simple and appreciated. For those with culinary skills, baking some

extra cookies, an extra loaf of bread, or even popcorn to share with a neighbor, friend or relative is almost always appreciated. Don't be surprised if such kindness comes back to you. Another easy to do thing, even if funds are limited, is to send a few dollars or more in an unmarked envelope to a charity that you know is doing good work. Add no return address, so they won't keep sending you letters asking for more. In sum, saying and doing kind things not only makes one feel better, but is quite likely to make people value you and may very well lead to friendships.

3) **Move**. Stop, drop and roll. No, not what we learned to do if we are on fire. Do the opposite: start, get up, and go. It's difficult to be depressed when you're on the go, and even getting up from your chair or bed will usually soon have you thinking of what to do next.

4) **Music** is powerful and most of us appreciate good music, whatever our musical tastes. Playing CD's, turning on a radio or TV music station, or going to YouTube to hear any kind of music we like should lift our spirits. Personally, I mute the advertising and turn the volume up when on You Tube. It's hard to be down when enjoying good music. Investment in a ten or twenty dollar set of computer speakers can enhance musical enjoyment. You Tube can also take us to places of interest nationally and around the world and can bring us talks and videos on all kinds of interesting subjects.

5) **Contact a friend**. Just talk.

6) **Smile**. Research shows that just turning the corners of our lips into a smile can make us happier and improve our mood. Doing the opposite, frowning or scowling is shown to affect us in a negative way.

7) **Write** a letter or email. This can be to a friend or to no one. The letter or email need not be sent. However, when composing it, it can be helpful to write down the things that are bothering you. Getting things down on paper or in email form can take them out of your mind and make them seem much more manageable. If they are things you need to do, you can prioritize them by assigning them numbers. Now that you have what's bothering you down on paper, it's easier to discuss them with a friend or with anyone you know willing to listen. Talking things out generally makes them seem smaller and more manageable. Besides, the person you talk to may have some good ideas that can make things seem not so difficult.

8) **Give thanks**. Take a several minute time out to give thanks for all that you have, not just for material possessions, but for your other God-given gifts like health, intelligence, your sense of humor, sunshine, children, grandchildren, etc. These gifts, too, are often helpful to write down.

8) **Pray**. Stop what you're doing to take a little time, be it only a minute, five minutes, or more to pray for others you know who are much worse off than yourself. Or, set aside a time during your day for prayer and stick to your intention. Prayer can be for yourself, for friends, for those in dire need, for those suffering persecution and death in faraway countries, and for those you may know who are going through hard times due to health or other reasons. Even if you should have only one good leg, pray for those who have none. Prayer as well as meditation are proven to be powerful antidotes to feelings of dejection.

Long Term Strategies

Ways to increase overall our measure of happiness

1) Humility. One of the major reasons we tend to get down on ourselves is because we feel we are not measuring up. We take clues from other people and think we should have a better job, a better home, and in general should have gotten farther along in life. The answer to our discontent is humility. Look around at all those we see. Look at the beggar on the street, at one who is severely handicapped, at a down's syndrome adult or an intellectually disabled person. Was their condition their fault? Unlikely. They did not receive the God given gifts you and I have received. On the other hand, many are smarter than we are, and know just how to be successful in life. Should we fault ourselves if we are not among them? Should the intellectually challenged person fault him or herself for not being smart? Of course not. Life can be complicated. We don't always make the best decisions. As for humility, perhaps author C.S. Lewis said it best: "Humility is not thinking less of yourself, it is thinking of yourself less." St. Paul also said it well: "Do nothing out of selfish ambition or vain conceit. Rather, in humility value others above yourselves, not looking to your own interests but each of you to the interests of others. (Philippians, 2:3-4)

2) **Forgiveness**. You and I are imperfect beings and so is everyone else. We all make mistakes, sometimes rather large ones. God is forgiving of mistakes; we Christians can rely on that. But do we?

Families are broken up by serious mistakes (sins). Unfaithfulness happens, either because of spur of the moment lust, or in longer term extra marital affairs. Who can forgive that? And should one forgive that? Likewise, family and extended family relationships can be severed by words better left unsaid. Example: "Can you believe what Uncle Harry said? He will never again be welcome back in this house!"

The hurt we feel when someone has betrayed us is long lasting. It affects not only our pride but also our self image as well as our emotional state. Our choice is to hold onto lasting bitterness toward that person or to eventually forgive. Psychologists tell us that retaining resentful feelings toward someone hurts us and takes away our peace. Christ, when asked about forgiveness said we should forgive seven times seven times. Certainly, he didn't mean to let people walk all over us.

If we can find it in our heart to forgive someone, even though that person doesn't deserve forgiveness, we will be the happier for it. This does not mean that in the future we will not stand up for our rights and for our beliefs. By forgiving, we are not implying that it's Ok to wrong us again.

And in truth, maybe we are the one who needs to ask for forgiveness. Especially if we honestly try never to fail in such a way again. In acknowledging our error, our mistake, our sin, we can have a clear conscience going forward whether or not the person we have offended accepts our contrition. However, if he or she **is** willing to forgive, there is a chance of starting over.

3) **Attending services.** Whether into religion or not, there are definite advantages to going to church. I know, not everyone may agree with all of a church's teachings. Go anyway. Church is a good place to give praise and thanks for our blessings and to ask the Lord for help with our personal needs and also for the needs of others we know. Church people are generally friendly, and if you partake in any of the many church activities or volunteer opportunities, you'll usually make friends. One recommendation: choose a mainstream church with a variety of believers rather than a small, focused church with very specific beliefs. Personally, I'm happy, born and raised a Catholic. However, we have good friends who are active members of other Christian churches. One couple actually spends several weeks each year doing missionary work in Africa. Impressive!

4) **Choose friends**. Not all friends are necessarily good friends although we may like them very much. We may share many memories with some of our old pals, buddies, or girlfriends. However, realistically, not all of these friends may be the best for our happiness. Some may tend to lead us into doing things that have the overall affect of making us unhappy. Overindulgence in drinking, experimenting with or using drugs, and meeting up with amoral women or men may bring us fleeting excitement but likely at the expense of long term happiness.

Rather, choose friends with whom we can enjoy all the good things in life—conversation, food, nature, entertainment, the great outdoors, etc. These friends will leave us with happy memories rather than hangovers and regret. In sum, it's good to remember the things, the events and the people with whom we have experienced good feelings and go back to them. It's best to minimize or break off completely with those friends whose overall effect is to leave us feeling down.

5) **Start a hobby** or a major undertaking. This can be a big positive in one's life. Put a good deal of thought into what you would like to do. Don't be put off by how long it might take. Instead, think of it as something you will enjoy doing in your spare time, but only when you feel like it. Make it something that will challenge you a bit

but not so difficult that you will give up in frustration. The ideal is something that you enjoy, that you will try to do well, and that you will in time look forward to completing. There should be no hurry, for it's a project to enjoy as you go, with no deadline for finishing. Whatever you decide to do, know that you can seek the advice of others who may have worked on a similar project. The possibilities are endless, and the fun is in doing it. People enjoy doing all kinds of things—oil painting, boat building, sewing projects, auto restoration, photo books, ceramics, crocheting, candle making, furniture building, wine making, gardening, leather crafts, magic tricks, model building, soap making, etc., etc. Whatever it is you're into, and these are only a few examples, there's sure to be many others doing the same or similar thing. It's fun to talk to and meet with likeminded people and get their ideas. Also, many things that are made are also appreciated as gifts. Whatever you may do, make sure it's something you enjoy.

6) **A worthy cause:** Volunteering to help a worthy endeavor can be satisfying in many ways. And, there are many different ways to help. Not everyone has extra time when raising a family. Especially when children are young, family needs to be the first priority. Even then, occasions arise when a school, church, community, or a neighborhood needs people to lend a

hand. When we give of our time to help, I believe we usually get back more than we give. We get it back in friendships formed, in the satisfaction of knowing we are able to help do a needed service, and in other ways. Especially, when we interact with those in need, assisting due to their health, poverty, or lack of knowledge, etc., we see how we are blessed compared with so many others.

Average lifespans have increased dramatically in the last 100 and even in the last 50 years. After children have left home, most of us can count on ten, twenty or thirty years of active life. Even after retirement, sometimes long after retirement, we can often retain the wisdom, stamina and ability to put our skills to use helping to make our community and our world a better place. There are so many volunteer opportunities, so many places we can fit in if we look, that it's a shame to sit in our recliner or rocking chair continuously watching television when we could spend at least a bit of our time doing good. And, perhaps one of the best consequences, is that we will feel good for doing it. We will become happier people.

Last but not least

Perhaps the best way to overcome our natural pride is to put things in perspective. By the way, the reason we need to work at overcoming pride is because we **are** great. We human beings have been given such tremendous powers and abilities that it can be hard for us not to take personal credit for our successes. However, it is God who created us with all of our superior traits and intelligence. Thank God, there is so much that each one of us is able to do. Nevertheless, it's good to remember that we are one of many billions of people who have come before us and many more billions who are likely to come after us. Where we were born and the time period we live in is beyond our control. We personally had nothing to do with it. Even our parents had nothing to do with where and when they were born. You and I just happen to be living in a certain place and time. That we are able to read is largely thanks to our place in history, for even two hundred years ago the vast majority of people of the world could not. Thomas Jefferson was far ahead of his time when in 1779 he proposed three years of free education for all free children. Note that he said nothing of educating slaves or indentured servants. We could say that, although he was ahead for his times, he was behind for our times.

There are so many other things for which all of us living in the twenty-first century can be thankful. For me personally, warm showers are big on my list. Even a hundred years ago they were not generally available and in some parts of the world are still not. Like my father-in-law before me, I am one of those who can say, "It's been over a year since I've taken a bath."

That we can communicate so easily with friends and loved ones in so many ways, is also thanks to the time in which we live. Even twenty years ago, one had to look for a telephone booth when away from home to make a call. That's real progress. Yes, for our education, for our comfortable life style, and for easy communication, we have much to be thankful.

However, we can have too much of a good thing. The ease of communication in particular lends itself to our being bombarded with news as well as ads that come via newspapers, internet and phones. To be good consumers we must be judicious in what we buy. Few can have it all. To increase our happiness, we need to take what is good from our society and click away from most of the bad news that can be so distressing. And yet, there are those times, when we do need to give attention to news, especially when it is happening around us.

Especially if we ourselves can be among those who by their good will can provide assistance to people or situations that can benefit from our help. In the end, happiness depends on us. If we focus on what is good rather than what is bad, if we are grateful for all that we have in this life, including those who care for us, and if we are generous in giving back, we will experience far more happiness in our lives.

If you enjoyed this book, or any of the ones listed in the following pages, please consider doing an Amazon review. Thank you!!

Limited Bibliography

Some works that were helpful in writing this book. I recommend them all.

Sonja Lyubomirsky: *The How of Happiness* (An in-depth work with hundreds of references)

Stefan Klein, PhD: *The Science of Happiness*

Fr. Jeffrey Kirby, STD: *Kingdom of Happiness*

Timothy Keller: *The Reason for God*

Peter Kreeft: *The God Who Loves You*

The Bible

Selected nonfiction and fiction by Tom Molnar on Amazon

Nonfiction

The Universe of God and Humanity

Some of the latest scientific findings are showing what Christians have long been aware, that God in creation has made a world of beautiful variety where all things fit together. Is evolution part of God's plan? Both the Bible and new science help to show the place of humanity in the not infrequently surprising universe made by our Creator.

Some Amazon reviews

I felt it was very thought provoking on many levels. I learned many new ideas that made me look at things more deeply.

This book helped me understand the mismatch between religion and science. It gave me a new insight between theological and philosophical thought. God is a mystery. The more we look the less we may see of God but at the same time the more we look with a true belief the more of God we see. God is more. Thanks for opening my mind and heart Tom. Great read!!!

Tom provides a clear introduction for a person to begin exploring the seeming contradiction between science and faith. His approach is clear and easy to follow. He is not afraid to tackle some of the more profound findings of modern science. He is thoughtful and respectful of everyone's beliefs and presents is own understanding of how to resolve these seeming contradictions. It is a nice beginning for a thoughtful, questioning person.

Jesus, Kind, Loving, Dangerous

The Pharisees realized right away that Jesus was a dangerous man. He was breaking their religious laws and keeping company with sinners. Ultimately, they had him crucified. We, however, often get the watered down version of Jesus depicted in books and movies. He doesn't seem dangerous to us, but he is. His life changing message is not one of following laws, but of transforming hearts.

64

This is a very enjoyable and thought provoking book. It is easy to read and comprehend. Mrs. Moorehead

This book makes you think and reflect. The author does a good job quoting Scripture and relating Jesus teaching to the times (time of Jesus and current day). David OMalley

Mary, the Girl who said Yes

When Mary said, yes, she didn't know how her answer would change her life. She didn't know her son would be born in a shelter for animals, or that she would have to flee a murderous king. Delving into her life shows a spirited and courageous woman, a fitting mother for Jesus, the man of God who changed history.

"I very much enjoyed your reflections on Mary," Bishop Dale Melczek

"A good overview of Mary and the times she lived in. Very nicely done." Rev. Joseph Hannon S.D.B.

"An interesting story told in a clever manner." Suzy Watts, book reviewer.

Fiction

Dark age Maiden

The most read of his novels thus far, Dark Age Maiden tells the true story of knights battling the invading

Saracen army, with a strong romantic thread and a feisty heroine.

Lady Carina is the favored daughter of the lord of the manor. She boldly refuses to marry the man he chose for her. Now, her father's fortress is under attack, and she escapes before dawn to reach the mysterious count he told her about. Before long, she finds herself caught up in the great Saracen attack on France as well as a very personal assault on her heart.

As the great Islamic army advances from Spain deep into Europe, Carina experiences the power of love, though she doesn't truly believe in love. But time is running out for her and for her country. The much feared Saracen army may soon be standing at the gate. Can Europe survive the assault, and what of Carina? Is she prepared to surrender her heart?

"From the moment I started reading this book it kept my interest and attention. Finished it in a day and a half. Loved all the characters.... Uberto, Count Giancarlo and of course Lady Carina. Beautiful love story and very easy to read. Can't wait for the sequel." Dave M (St. Mike's)

"This was a very lovely story and YES, I would definitely enjoy reading many sequels." Lilia L

"I loved reading story. I am so very glad to have come across your book. I look forward to a sequel. You are one of my two favorite writers." Linda W"

"Thank you for this beautiful story. It started well in the beginning and ended very well too. You are a creative writer and I would like to see more of your wonderful creations." Romina A

"So glad that I added your book to my library. Really good read! Thank you!" Penny Z

"Great, great book. I love all the history. Bravo." Granny Y

Swept Away

Swept Away draws from Civil War records, from accounts of life in the times, and from a true love story. It brings to life a novel of Jenny, a girl turning 18 as the war begins. It finds her caught up in the love of a man for whom she is only his "best friend." When Daniel leaves to fight for the South, Jenny's small town and her father's farm are soon occupied by hated Yankee soldiers, one of whom, a captain, has the audacity to smile at her.

As the war intensifies, Jenny will find courage to do things she never thought she would do, and she will see things she never thought she would see. Swept Away brings home the reality of war as well as life as it was lived in rural America. It is Jenny's story, one of love, tragedy and beginning anew.

Since I am not a lover of history, I was very impressed by the interest the characters kept me involved in the story. I enjoyed this very much. JBehr

"tender love story" I enjoyed reading this story, especially the historical details. It certainly shows the hardships and sacrifices endured by so many during the Civil War. P. Negovetich

P.S. If you wondered about the short saying on the front cover, it's taken from St. Paul's second letter to the Corinthians, chapter 7, verse 4.

www.ingramcontent.com/pod-product-compliance
Lightning Source LLC
Chambersburg PA
CBHW071931020426

42331CB00010B/2821

* 9 7 8 1 7 3 4 3 5 9 3 2 9 *